For Peter
Peace and friendship.
Michael Longley

"this evil thing..."

Chairman of the No-Conscription Fellowship
Clifford Allen's description of military conscription.

This Evil Thing: a play for one actor

by

Michael Mears

**49Knights
Independent Publishing House
Edinburgh & Cambridge**

© 2017 by Michael Mears

Rights of performance by amateurs are controlled by the author, Michael Mears, and he, or his authorised agents, issue licences to amateurs on payment of a fee. **It is an infringement of the Copyright to give any performance or public reading of these plays before the fee has been paid and the license issued.**

The Royalty Fee is subject to contract, and subject to variation, at the sole discretion of the author, Michael Mears.

The basic fee for each and every performance by amateurs in the British Isles is available upon request from michaelmears.org.

The Professional Rights in this playscript are controlled by the author, Michael Mears, who bears sole responsibility should there be found within any infringement upon the personal rights of any third party, including, without limitation, claims in defamation, privacy, copyright, or trademark.

The publication of this play does not imply that it is necessarily available for performance by amateurs or professionals, either in the British Isles or Overseas. Amateurs and professionals considering a production are strongly advised, in their own interests, to apply to the appropriate agents for consent prior to starting rehearsals or booking a venue.

The fact that a play is published by 49Knights, Independent Publishing House, Edinburgh & Cambridge, does not indicate that performance rights are available, or that 49Knights controls such rights.

Original Kitchener image courtesy of the Library of Congress, this version copyright Michael Mears 2016.

ISBN: 978-0-9931975-6-7

Please see page 6 for further copyright information.

by Michael Mears

This Evil Thing

First printing of the first edition

This Evil Thing by Michael Mears

Foreword by Rosamunde Hutt

Text edited by Dan Lentell

Cover layout and incidental artwork by Carys Boughton

Original portrait of the author by Catherine Shakespeare-Lane

Typesetting by John Tiratsoo

Further information about plays, licensing, current productions and tours can be found at **michaelmears.org**.

COPYRIGHT INFORMATION

(See also page 4)

This play is fully protected under the Copyright Laws of the British Commonwealth of Nations, the United States of America and all countries of the Berne and Universal Copyright Conventions.

All rights including Stage, Motion Picture, Radio, Television, Public Reading, and Translation into Foreign Languages, are strictly reserved.

No part of this publication may be lawfully reproduced in ANY form or by any means - photocopying, typescript, recording (including video-recording), manuscript, electronic, mechanical or otherwise - or be transmitted or stored in a retrieval system, without prior permission.

Licences for amateur productions are issued subject to the understanding that it shall be made clear in all advertising matter that the audience will witness an amateur performance; that the names of the authors of the plays shall be included in all programmes and that the integrity of the author's work will be preserved.

The Royalty Fee is subject to contract and subject to variation at the sole discretion of the author, Michael Mears.

NB. A licence issued to perform this play does not include permission to use any incidental music specified in this copy. Such permission must be separately obtained from the appropriate agent.

VIDEO-RECORDING OF AMATEUR PRODUCTIONS

Please note that the copyright laws governing video-recording are extremely complex and that it should not be assumed that any play may be video-recorded for whatever purpose without first obtaining the permission of the appropriate agents. The fact that these plays are published by 49Knights, Independent Publishing House, Edinburgh & Cambridge, does not indicate that video rights are available or that 49Knights controls such rights.

FOREWORD

It was with great joy in early 2016 that I accepted Michael's offer to direct This Evil Thing. From March to June Michael and I met every now and then to sharpen and develop his play. We had the advantage that as the researcher and writer he was deeply engaged with the material and could bring all the knowledge that he had accrued to the playing of the roles.

Our starting point in the final stage of dramaturgy was discovering where he could 'show' not 'tell'. First we needed to find out how to depict the world of the play. We looked at photographs and paintings by artists from the First World War. We saw haunting repeated images of the trenches. Wood was everywhere, propping up flimsy structures. There were pallets to traverse across; sandbags protecting the soldiers from mud and water; numbers stamped onto boxes carrying first aid, food and weapons, destined for the Somme. The brutalising physical effort struck home, stretcher carriers running under gunfire, men tunnelling deep into the earth.

The Conscientious Objectors themselves were far from idle, engaged in back breaking war work or, when imprisoned, carving their initials or those of loved ones into the stone walls of their cells in Richmond Castle. We drew on all these images to create our world.

Designer Mark Friend suggested we try out some wooden crates and we hired seven from the National Theatre for an exploratory Playday before rehearsals began. These crates would become all that we required, the despatch box, a garden bench, a desk in Number 10, a filing cabinet, an instrument of torture, a cell, a cemetery, all to be arranged by Michael into significant stage pictures.

This was a piece to be driven by the energy and physical hard work of the performer. No revolving stages or intricate costume changes for us! Just planks (or crates) and a passion. Seven became nine. No need for any other scenery. The crates would do it all. But into this workmanlike environment we highlighted little touches of elegance or defiance, a much loved pipe, a beautiful teacup, a red flag, white hankies flying high – these not as a sign of surrender but of joy, hope and solidarity.

Michael and I were 'on tour' as we rehearsed, finding the visual physical journeys of the staging in the Rosemary Branch Theatre, where sunlight flooded into our high room above the pub, or in the basement of Room One, near Old Street, an intense concentrated space. In the afternoons we would retire to Michael's home and in the sitting room would dig deep into the specific characterisation of each character, ensuring that each of the multitude of people Michael would play had his or her own physical traits, particular tone of voice or regional accent.

Who was bold, commanding, charismatic? Who was gently persuasive or ironically witty? Who was filled with longing and regret?

Each character had a name and a distinct story, drawn from the figures we had read about. And at the heart of the story we got to know the two Berts, Bert Brocklesby, whose history I read every morning in a park outside the Rosemary Branch before the building opened, or Bertrand Russell whose words feel so ahead of their time it is uncanny. Michael had old recordings of him speaking and his voice filled Michael's kitchen and took us right back to the early 20th century.

The evocative soundscape for the play was created by Mark Noble, who created the atmosphere of draughty meeting rooms, London's Bishopsgate Hall, the family home, the Houses of Parliament and the French sea coast. The naturalistic sounds of domestic and epic interiors and exteriors were shot through with abstract and haunting harmonies building to the life-giving song of the skylarks at the end (the skylarks having been recorded by Michael on his iPhone on a trip to north Norfolk). Mark was regularly present in rehearsals so was able to help orchestrate the pace and intensity of the material with clever and sensitive editing.

Zoe Spurr's lighting defined the story's spaces and heightened key storytelling moments, the lighting becoming more fluid and atmospheric as the play progressed, capturing the profundity and pain of the choices made by the Conscientious Objectors, the struggle with conscience, and with baffled loved ones, and the aching weariness of long years spent in prison even when the war was over.

Add to this bursts of wartime songs, both patriotic and ironic, a hymn conducted by Methodist choirmaster Bert, cheering crowds celebrating the Armistice, all sung by composer Helen Chadwick and her merry band, and our world was complete. Michael envisaged a beautiful female voice lamenting for the loss of life and honouring the sacrifices made and Helen's voice soars at the close of the play with a piece that echoes the sound of The Last Post.

We did two Previews in London to friends whom we knew would provide a helpful critical eye and fine-tuned our presentation after their comments. But it was clear that they loved the show and were deeply moved by the material so, fingers crossed, and bags packed, we set off to Edinburgh for the Festival.

Safely ensconced in the magnificent Freemasons Hall on George Street Michael then performed for four weeks to captivated audiences of all ages, including many Quakers whose predecessors had so courageously stood up to hostile authorities, and at times broken apart their very own families for their belief in peace, not war.

It was a privilege to be immersed in the world of the Conscientious Objectors during the summer of 2016, 100 years after Conscription came into law, and to bring to life their stories with the prodigious skills and golden talents of actor - writer Michael Mears.

–Rosamunde Hutt
Director, *This Evil Thing*

INTRODUCTION

"My dear mother and sister, I am now confined in a pit which started at the surface at three feet by two, and tapers off to two feet six inches by fifteen. Water was struck, but they continued digging until it was ten feet deep. There is no room to walk about and sitting is impossible. The sun beats down and through the long day there are only the walls of clay to look at..."

A letter written from someone languishing in Guantanamo Bay? Or in a cell in Saudi Arabia? No. This particular incarceration occurred at Cleethorpes on Humberside, in 1917. The victim was James Brightmore, a solicitor's clerk from Manchester, and a conscientious objector.

When I read this, and other accounts of brutality inflicted by the British Army on those young British men whose consciences would not permit them to take part in the First World War, I felt moved, as an actor and playwright, to tell their story in some shape or form.

Thanks to the wonderful library at Friends House in London, and a number of excellent books on the subject, including David Boulton's *Objection Overruled*, Jo Vellacott's *Bertrand Russell and The Pacifists*, (now reprinted by Spokesman Books under the title *Conscientious Objection*), John W. Graham's *Conscription and Conscience*, and more recently, Cyril Pearce's *Comrades In Conscience*, I was made aware of the extraordinary resistance that was put up to the introduction of military conscription, and the harsh challenges facing those men who refused to answer the summons to barracks. I learnt of the intricate network of helpers and supporters in places high and low, and the organisations that helped them in their struggle, preeminent amongst them, surely, the No Conscription Fellowship, founded by Fenner Brockway in late 1914. And I was filled with admiration for the tireless efforts of those supporters, one of whom was the eminent mathematician and philosopher Bertrand Russell.

There are many other heroes and heroines who played their role in these epic events, too numerous to list here, but the remarkable

Catherine Marshall must be mentioned, for her untiring, meticulous and ingenious work for the N-C F, and who became Russell's prime associate in the organisation as the war progressed; and Clifford Allen, the agnostic socialist and quietly charismatic chairman of the N-C F, who Russell replaced when it became Allen's turn to be arrested for refusing to report to barracks. And, of course, the 16,000 plus C.O.s, who endured endless indignities, contempt and harsh treatment at the hands of the military.

The C.O.s came from all walks of life, some were political objectors, there were many religious objectors, others objected simply on ethical or humanist grounds. And within the movement that sprang up, epitomised by the N-C F, there were many shades of opinion as to how far they should carry their protest. Some were only opposed to killing and were prepared to help the war effort in any other way – to take on any kind of 'alternative service' or 'work of national importance'. But a hard core of C.O.s baulked at this compromise, believing war in itself was utterly wrong and wicked, and refused to do anything at all to help the war effort. These men became known as 'absolutists'.

This Evil Thing focuses on the story of one C.O. in particular - Bert Brocklesby, a young Methodist schoolteacher from south Yorkshire, whose 'absolutist' stance led him inexorably to a parade ground in France and the prospect of execution.

Bert's memoir, *Escape From Paganism*, is unpublished but I was able to read it at the Friends House Library. And in 2016 I was lucky enough to meet his grand-daughter, Jill Gibbon, who along with the remaining family members, gave me her blessing for this project and for telling Bert's story. I am deeply indebted to them all.

The story of the First World War conscientious objectors and those who supported them is certainly a shocking one at times, but ultimately I find it an intensely inspiring one, blazing the trail as it does for the rights of freedom of conscience and thought. Or as the words on the Conscientious Objectors' Memorial Stone in Tavistock Square, London express it:

> "To all those who have established and are maintaining
> The right to refuse to kill,
> Their foresight and courage give us hope."

Inspiring though their story is, throughout all my research and writing I became increasingly aware of a question poking me, prodding at me, haunting me: how would *I* have responded if I'd been a young man in 1914? How would any of us have responded?

This Evil Thing

First performed in August 2016 at the New Town Theatre, Edinburgh.

Written and performed by Michael Mears

Directed by Rosamunde Hutt
Sound design and recording by Mark Noble
Set design by Mark Friend
Crates custom built by Taylor and Foley Propmakers
    (www.taylorandfoley.co.uk)
Lighting design by Zoe Spurr
Stage manager in rehearsals Jane Andrews
Voice and accent coaching by Kay Welch
Bert Brocklesby's jacket, and the military cap, plus certain other props were kindly loaned by the Royal Academy of Dramatic Art

I Didn't Raise My Boy To Be A Soldier sung by Helen Chadwick
Original recording sung by the Peerless Quartet
Violin played by Sally Davies (sallydaviesmusic.co.uk)
Accordion played by Martina Schwarz (www.martinaschwarz.net)
Nearer My God To Thee, If I Die and other songs in the play sung by Helen Chadwick, James Lailey, Shaun Chambers, Rebecca Thorn, Martina Schwarz and Michael Mears
Extract from *If I Die* composed by Helen Chadwick,
    text by Pablo Neruda
Lament composed and sung by Helen Chadwick

The play lasts approximately 75 mins.

This Evil Thing is dedicated to Jill Gibbon, granddaughter of Bert Brocklesby.

Note on the text: SFX = sound and/or lighting effect.

CHARACTERS WHO APPEAR ON STAGE

PRINCIPAL CHARACTERS

The Narrator
James Brightmore, Conscientious Objector (C.O.)
Bert Brocklesby, C.O.
Bertrand Russell, mathematician and philosopher
Fenner Brockway, C.O. and founder of the No-Conscription Fellowship
Annie Wainwright, Bert Brocklesby's fiancee
John Brocklesby, Bert's father
Herbert Henry Asquith, Prime Minister (1908-1916)
Clifford Allen, C.O. and Chairman of the No-Conscription Fellowship
Philip Snowden, Independent Labour Party MP
Jack Gray, C.O.
Norman Gaudie, C.O.
Catherine Marshall, Honorary Secretary of the No-Conscription Fellowship

OTHER CHARACTERS

Canon H. J. Scrine
A Major
A Welsh miner
A Scots docker
The Under-Secretary for War
Mr. Wilson, a member of Conisbrough Methodist Chapel congregation
Mrs. Appleyard, a member of the congregation
Mr. Booth, a member of the congregation
Mr. Shenton, a member of the congregation
Three Conservative MPs in favour of conscription
Harold Bing, C.O.
A Socialist C.O.

An Atheist C.O.
Commanding Officer at Shore Camp
An Army Sergeant at Richmond Castle
A Lieutenant at Richmond Castle
An Army Sergeant in charge of Jack Gray
Commanding Officer at Henriville, Boulogne
An Adjutant at Henriville, Boulogne
Leonard and Howard, two C.O.s in France
Gordon and Stephen, two C.O.s at Dyce Camp, Aberdeen
A Sour Warder at Maidstone Prison
A Judge
A 2nd Warder at Maidstone Prison

CHARACTERS WHOSE VOICES ARE RECORDED

A Pathe Newsreel Newscaster
Angry MPs in the House of Commons
Five Members of the Doncaster Tribunal
Three Tribunal Chairmen from different localities
A Policeman
The Speaker of the House of Commons
A Police Officer at West Riding Police Court
Major-General Wyndham Childs
An Officer in charge of a firing squad
The Prime Minister's Secretary
An Army Sergeant at Henriville, Boulogne
A Sergeant-Major at Henriville, Boulogne
A C.O. at Henriville parade ground
Scots Warder at Dyce Camp, Aberdeen

*****

The action of the play takes place at various times between 1902 to 1919, though the Narrator is telling the story at the present time.

The action takes place in various locations throughout Britain, and in Boulogne, France.

by Michael Mears

[*Nine wooden crates, pallets and trunks are lined up around the edge of the stage. There are also two hessian sacks, some rope, and a primitive wooden coat-stand.*

NARRATOR appears. He takes one of the crates from upstage, removes a plank from it and places the crate centre-stage, then stands on it unsteadily. He is now James Brightmore, 19 years old, composing a letter on a cigarette packet, using a tiny pencil stub.

The light is very bright and a high insistent note is faintly heard underneath.]

BRIGHTMORE: Shore Camp, Cleethorpes. June 24th 1917. My dear mother and sister, this is the best stuff I can find to write what may be my last letter. I am now confined in a pit, ten feet deep, which started at the surface at three feet by two, and tapers off to two feet six inches by fifteen. The bottom is full of water, and I have to stand on two strips of wood all day long just above the water line. There is no room to walk about and sitting is impossible.

[*The high note grows more insistent, the light from above grows brighter.*]

The sun beats down and through the long day there are only the walls of clay to look at. I wish I could see your letters! I could be reassured or know your wishes. As it is, I feel sentenced to death - knowing that within a few days I could be sent to France... and shot.

[*The insistent note fades away. The man steps off the crate and addresses the audience.*]

NARRATOR: James Brightmore was a solicitor's clerk from Manchester. He was also a conscientious objector.

[NARRATOR *tips one of the crates on its end, sits on it and becomes Brightmore's commanding OFFICER.*]

OFFICER: You've already served eight months in prison for disobeying orders, and as you show no sign of ceasing your pointless protest I'm now going to sentence you to solitary confinement.

[*He is interrupted.*]

Yes, Corporal? What d'you mean, there's no cell available? Well then find somewhere else... Dig a pit if necessary!

[NARRATOR *stands and addresses the audience again.*]

NARRATOR: It was after Brightmore had spent a week in the pit that a sympathetic soldier, at great risk to himself, dropped down a pencil stub and cigarette packet, on which Brightmore wrote his letter home.

[SFX *booming artillery fire and shelling fades up. He opens one of the wooden trunks and pulls out two photograph frames, showing them to the audience.*]

NARRATOR: My grandfather, William Mears, fought in the First World War. My dad, Ron Mears, fought in the Second World War.

My best friend at school, Scott Dodkins, went on to Sandhurst to have a successful career in the Army as an officer; and it was

> Scott who mocked me mercilessly about my pencil case...

[NARRATOR *takes out a pencil case from the trunk.*]

> ...on which, at the age of 15, I'd written in Tipp-Ex, "WAR IS ILLOGICAL!"

[*Calls up to the control box.*]

> Could we cut that sound effect, please?

[SFX *of gunfire snaps off.*]

> I don't know where my pacifist gene came from, if there is such a thing as a pacifist gene. But what I do know is that my pacifism has never been tested – not truly tested. Not in the way that James Brightmore's was tested. Or Bert Brocklesby's.

[NARRATOR *approaches the audience.*]

> Has someone got a coin, please? A two pence piece or fifty pence piece would be good.

[NARRATOR *takes a coin from an audience member.*] [1]

> Thank you. You will get it back, I promise.

[NARRATOR *stacks two of the crates to suggest a bedroom window.*]

> When war was declared in 1914, three years before this pit was dug, the British Army was completely dependent on volunteers.

---

1 It's not happened so far, but if no one in the audience had a coin I would resort to using the emergency one I'd put in the bottom of my pocket just in case! - MM

[NARRATOR 'opens' the window and is now BERT Brocklesby, looking down on to the street below.]

BERT: Look at them all... Queueing up round the square and halfway down the Sheffield Road... There are my brothers! Harold! Phil! [He waves down to them.] How can I not be part of this?

[NARRATOR pulls out a jacket from inside one of the crates and slips it on.]

NARRATOR: Bert Brocklesby was a twenty-five year old schoolteacher, living in the south Yorkshire town of Conisbrough. He was also choirmaster and lay preacher at his local Methodist chapel.

BERT: But what about the Sixth Commandment? What about my belief that the Lord's called me to work for His Kingdom, not to go about destroying His children?

If I believe, as I do, that God controls everything, then surely he can control the spin of a coin tossed in the air.

[BERT holds up the coin and stares at it.]

So I'll ask Him – I'll ask Him for a plain yes or no – should I volunteer? Heads will signify that God wishes me... to keep my head, not to volunteer.

[BERT tosses the coin and catches it on the back of his hand.]

Heads. Can't make up my mind on just one toss, though.

[Tosses again.]

> Tails. Right. This is the decider.

[Tossing the coin.]

> Heads.

[BERT returns the coin to the audience member who lent it to him.]

> Thank you.

[BERT hesitates.]

> Two to one though. I don't find that very convincing.

[BERT takes the coin back.]

[Tossing the coin again.]

> Heads.

[Tossing again.]

> Heads.

[Tossing again.]

> Heads.

[Tossing again.]

> Heads. Six to one? That's pretty persuasive.

[BERT moves towards the audience member again, then swerves away again.]

But the Lord had twelve disciples. What if I toss twelve times in all, once for each of them? I realise this is not a method a maturer judgment would recommend.

[*Tossing again.*]

Heads.

[*Tossing again.*]

Heads.

[*Tossing again.*]

Heads.

[*Tossing again.*]

Heads.

[*Tossing again.*]

Heads.

[*Silence.*]

11 to 1. That 'one' was Judas, I imagine. Well. This only confirms what I know in my heart.

[BERT *pockets the coin and stares out of the window again.*]

I just pray the Army doesn't run out of volunteers.

[SFX *a fanfare and Pathe-news-style music erupts into the space. The brisk, clipped voice of a* NEWSCASTER *is heard. Meanwhile* NARRATOR *removes* BERT's *jacket, puts the photo frames back into the trunk, and takes items of clothing out of one of the hessian sacks.]*

NEWSCASTER: The year is 1902 when the National Service League is founded - pushing for a programme of military conscription. Its first president is the Duke of Wellington and early supporters include Rudyard Kipling. The Church too is well represented, the Bishop of Chester is one of its founder-members, and in one of the League's leaflets Canon H.J. Scrine declares...

[NARRATOR turns to face the audience wearing a dog-collar.]

SCRINE: War is not murder, as some fancy. The fighting and killing are not the essence of it, but are the accidents, though the inseparable accidents; and even these are mainly purged of savagery and transfigured into devotion. War is not murder, but sacrifice; which is the soul of Christianity.

NEWSCASTER: But even with the support of Lord Northcliffe's Daily Mail, there are plenty of voices speaking out against conscription.

[NARRATOR moves upstage, in an officer's hat.]

MAJOR: The most valuable thing for an army is not quantity but quality.

[NARRATOR waves a cloth cap.]

WELSH MINER: Moreover, if Britain introduces conscription, it will alarm our neighbours and could well accelerate the arms race!

[NARRATOR *puts the cloth cap on and shifts some crates.*]

SCOTS DOCKER: Besides which, Britain's defences are already safeguarded by its enormous, growing and costly navy!

NEWSCASTER: But most importantly, as the Under-Secretary for War declares in the House of Commons...

UNDER-SEC'Y: Compulsion is foreign to the British nation, to the British character and to the genius of our people.

FIRST MP: [*Recorded.*] Hear, hear!

NEWSCASTER: By August 1914, the mood in the country is predominantly against conscription, although one of Britain's most eminent mathematicians and philosophers fears that that mood cannot last much longer.

[NARRATOR *moves into a gap between the crates upstage, holding a pipe. He is Bertrand RUSSELL.*]

RUSSELL: The evening before war is declared I find myself walking the streets of London, noticing the cheering crowds, making myself sensitive to the emotions of passers-by. I have always imagined, what most pacifists contend, that wars are forced upon a reluctant population by despotic and Machiavellian governments. But during this and the following days I discover to my amazement that the average man and woman is delighted at the prospect of war, revels in the anticipation of carnage. I need to revise my views on human nature.

NARRATOR: Bertrand Russell was 42, so if conscription was brought in, it's unlikely he'd be called up. But younger pacifists, like Fenner Brockway...

BROCKWAY: Believe some kind of pre-emptive action has to be taken!

[*NARRATOR puts on spectacles and becomes Fenner BROCKWAY. His voice is first heard recorded, then we see him speaking live.*]

BROCKWAY: [*Recorded.*] Although conscription may not be so imminent as the press suggests, it would perhaps be well for men of enlistment age who are not prepared to take the part of a combatant in the war, whatever the penalty for refusing, to band themselves together so that we may know our strength...

BROCKWAY: [*Live.*] Write to me at the address below. Yours etc. Fenner Brockway.

[*A doorbell sounds. BROCKWAY dashes upstage and returns with the second hessian sack, which is full of letters, and tips them onto the floor.*]

The return posts bring hundreds of replies, heralding the birth of the No-Conscription Fellowship.

[*BROCKWAY sorts through the letters.*]

Including in its ranks: Quakers, Socialists, International Workers of the World, anarchists, atheists, and many other political and religious objectors. Our chairman is the socialist agnostic Clifford Allen. And on our national committee... Bertrand Russell!

NARRATOR: If I'd been a young man in 1914, would I have joined the No-Conscription Fellowship? Absolutely!

[NARRATOR 'posts' his own letter into the sack. SFX of a choir singing the final verse of 'Nearer My God to Thee'. NARRATOR puts BERT's jacket on again.]

NARRATOR: One of the religious objectors who joins the Fellowship is Bert Brocklesby...

[A crate becomes a pulpit and BERT steps onto it to address the congregation at Conisbrough Methodist Chapel.]

BERT: Yesterday I came across some words by Dr. Alfred Salter, words which struck me forcibly and which I'd like to share with you. He says that if our religion is the Christian religion, and we want to know what we should do under any given circumstances, we must ask ourselves, what would Christ do in our place? In the matter of this war, would Christ answer the Prime Minister's call, make himself proficient in arms, dress up in uniform, and hurry to the continent to beat the Germans off? Christ in khaki, out in France, thrusting His bayonet into the body of a German workman! Can we picture that?

[Somebody angrily interrupts him, but he carries on.]

Of course - of course we can't picture it - that picture is an impossible one and we all know it. And Dr. Salter goes on to say that that settles the matter for him. He cannot uphold the war, even on its supposedly defensive side, and he cannot, therefore, advise anyone else to take part in what he believes to be wrong and wicked for himself.

[*More interruptions.*]

But he then – but – please, may I finish – but he then asks, what will be the consequences of such a policy for himself? If he refuses to fight or support measures of defence, it's possible he may be shot by the authorities as guilty of treason. Very well, he says. Rather than kill a German lad with whom he has no conceivable quarrel, he is prepared to be shot himself. Prepared to be shot himself.

[*He steps down from the pulpit and is accosted by members of the congregation.*]

MR. WILSON: You had no business to preach that sermon tonight! It's not Methodist doctrine!

MRS. APPLEBY: He only preached it because he's too frightened to go himself.

Why don't you take this, Mr. Brocklesby... [*She presents BERT with a white feather.*] ... and wear it in your lapel.

MR. BOOTH: Listen, young man, why haven't you joined up yet? The Commandments? Oh bugger the Commandments!

[*They leave him as ANNIE Wainwright, Bert's fiancée, steps forward.*]

ANNIE: Bert!

BERT: Annie – hallo, my love.

[*They kiss.*]

ANNIE: You were very brave to say those things in your sermon, Bert –... [*She notices the white feather.*] Who gave you that white feather? You're not a coward. You're standing up for what you believe in, Bert. That's brave.

[*MR. SHENTON appears and interrupts them.*]

MR. SHENTON: Did you say brave, Miss Wainwright? My son was injured at Neuve Chapelle last year, could have died, and he has the gall to get up in a pulpit and preach that it's wrong and wicked? Makes me sick to my stomach! And don't you have a brother Gilbert, serving in France as we speak, Miss Wainwright?

ANNIE: I do, yes.

MR. SHENTON: Well then. Don't know how you can be engaged to such a man!

[*MR. SHENTON exits. Bert's father, JOHN Brocklesby, appears.*]

JOHN: Bert!

BERT: Father.

JOHN: You don't make things easy for me, do you, son, preaching sermons like that. Hallo, Annie love. Now look, I know you won't consider the Army Medical Corps, but what about the Quakers? The Quakers are requesting volunteers for their Friends

Ambulance Unit – and they're not attached to the Army in any way – that would surely suit you?

BERT: It troubles me, father.

JOHN: What does? Helping the wounded? Surely, that's a worthy task to undertake?

BERT: It's not that straightforward. The problem is ... what they do once they're recovered. If the unit I'm with is simply helping the injured get strong again so they can return to the front to resume their killing, then...

I know! I know it's run by the Quakers, father, you've made that point! But I'm sorry. I don't think I can.

[SFX *fanfare and Pathe-news-style music erupts into the space again. As before, NEWSCASTER's voice is recorded.*]

NEWSCASTER: In the first three months of the war, with volunteers coming forward at the rate of 300,000 a month, the case for conscription seemed irrelevant. But by Christmas it's becoming all too apparent that the war will be a long drawn-out struggle devouring vast amounts of manpower. In the Spring of 1915 the Liberal Government is brought down; and on the 19th May, Prime Minister Henry Asquith announces...

[*NARRATOR briefly becomes ASQUITH.*]

ASQUITH: The formation of a Coalition.

NEWSCASTER: ...a coalition which includes significant members of the Conservative Party.

[SFX *of battle. As the lights dim and flicker,* NARRATOR *picks up a wooden pallet and becomes a stretcher-bearer, moving through the battlefield.*]

NEWSCASTER: By September 1915, with the casualty toll now over... three... hundred... and eighty... thousand...

[*The number 380,000 is echoed around the auditorium.* NARRATOR *puts down the stretcher.*]

...with the casualty toll now over 380,000, one Tory backbencher after another rises to put what they believe is the irrefutable case for conscription.

[NARRATOR *now becomes various MPs, waving order papers as if in Parliament.*]

FIRST MP: Conscription is justified not only by the pressing necessity of having more men, but on the better and higher ground of equality of service.

SECOND MP: Hear, hear! The working classes would far prefer universal service to a voluntary system, under which it is only the willing horse who goes, while the loafers and shirkers stay at home!

THIRD MP: Hear, hear! And to set an example, those who are wealthy should make the ultimate sacrifice for King and Country, of giving up the luxury of motor travel and immediately sending their chauffeurs into the army!

[THIRD MP *stands and parps a car-horn, which is augmented by SFX of the hooting of a battalion of car-horns.*

Explosions are heard, the rattle of machine-gun fire, the boom of artillery, as crates and pallets are shifted around the stage by NARRATOR; *the battlefield sounds then fade out, leaving the sound of birdsong and a single violin playing 'In an English Country Garden.'*

A bright summer's day. NARRATOR *is now holding Bertrand* RUSSELL's *pipe.*]

RUSSELL: I'm staying with my lover Ottoline Morrell, and her husband the Liberal MP, Philip Morrell, at their country home in Oxfordshire.[2] I've just been bathing stark naked in their pond, when I find Henry Asquith on the bank as I get out.

[*He whips out a handkerchief, and swiftly covers his manhood.*]

The quality of dignity which should characterize a meeting between the Prime Minister and a pacifist is somewhat lacking on this occasion.

[NARRATOR *interrupts the scene by approaching the audience.*]

NARRATOR: But what do they talk about? Russell doesn't say. Was there a conversation between them which ran something like this?

---

2 Lady Ottoline Violet Anne Morrell (1873-1938) was a great-great-niece of the Duke of Wellington, a society hostess and celebrated patron of artists including Aldous Huxley, Siegfried Sassoon, T.S. Eliot and D.H. Lawrence. During their long affair, Ottoline and Bertrand Russell exchanged more than 2000 letters. Like Russell, she was passionately opposed to the war. - MM

ASQUITH: How's the atmosphere at Cambridge?

RUSSELL: Chilly.

ASQUITH: Yes. I gather you don't have many sympathisers there.

NARRATOR: [*Interrupting.*] Imagine them both on a bench by the pond. [*He upends a pallet to act as a bench for them to sit on.*] Russell just in a towel, soaking up the sun after his swim; the Prime Minister, a keen golfer, in plus-fours, not having changed for supper yet...

[*NARRATOR sits on the bench and portrays both men.*]

RUSSELL: I'm made to feel like a traitor; the older dons getting more hysterical by the day, avoiding me at high table, as if I'm the sole reason the war hasn't been won yet. Do you have a match? This pipe's going out.

ASQUITH: I don't, I'm afraid.

RUSSELL: Believe me, Prime Minister, I desire the defeat of Germany as ardently as any retired colonel. Love of England is very nearly the strongest emotion I possess – and having to set it aside at this time, well, it's not an easy thing to renounce, I can tell you, but I've no choice. We shouldn't be at war. And such a trivial war, too.

ASQUITH: Trivial?

RUSSELL: No great principle is at stake...

ASQUITH: I profoundly disagree.

RUSSELL: No great human purpose is involved on either side. It's mere barbarity. I mean, the use of gas, for goodness sake! Is this the way in which the finest scientific brains in Europe are now being employed, to concoct the most lethally disabling substances known to man?

ASQUITH: If I might remind you, Russell, it was the Germans who used gas first.

RUSSELL: Does it not occur to any of you to sue for peace?

ASQUITH: Now? After so many thousands have died? What a climb-down that would be. A disgrace! No. We have to see it through.

RUSSELL: For the sake of the financiers, I suppose, for the sake of the arms manufacturers, for the sake –

[*This brings ASQUITH to his feet.*]

ASQUITH: I say now what I said to the House the day after war was declared: that our country is fighting neither for aggression, nor for the advancement of our own selfish interests, but for <u>*principles*</u> whose maintenance is vital to the civilised world.

RUSSELL: But you're destroying the civilised world! The civilised world will not recover from this onslaught for decades. Decades! Shouldn't we have evolved by now to a point where we can resolve our disputes in a manner which doesn't involve such ghastly carnage? What are you laughing at!

[*Beat.*]

ASQUITH: It's difficult talking about such things to a mathematician wearing nothing but a towel.

RUSSELL: It's difficult talking about such things to a Prime Minister wearing plus-fours.

[*Pause. ASQUITH sits back down.*]

ASQUITH: Well, I'd no idea I'd be debating the war.

[SFX *The violin is heard again.*]

But listen... Russell... there is something I'd like to ask. I gather from Ottoline that you're getting involved with the No-Conscription Fellowship.

RUSSELL: I am involved, Prime Minister, yes.

ASQUITH: Why are you all so certain there'll be conscription?

RUSSELL: If casualties continue at the current rate, what other option will be open to you?

ASQUITH: Tell me, Russell... *if* conscription were to be brought in, how many would refuse it in your estimation?

[*RUSSELL considers this for a moment.*]

RUSSELL: Ten thousand.

ASQUITH: That many?

RUSSELL: At least. That's rather a lot of prison cells you'll have to find.

ASQUITH: And what do you think would pacify them – if you'll pardon the pun?

RUSSELL: You can't force a man to murder against his will, Prime Minister. There will have to be a conscience clause.

[*The lights darken. SFX of a Pathe-style newsreel. NEWSCASTER's recorded voice is heard as a drum-roll starts, building in volume. ASQUITH collects a tumbler of whisky from behind a crate, on which he sits, perusing papers.*]

NEWSCASTER: By Christmas 1915, the British casualty toll is 528, 227. On December the 27th and December the 28th, the Cabinet meets to discuss the crisis. And at the start of the New Year, on January 5th, 1916, the Prime Minister rises to address the House.

[*The drum-roll reaches its crescendo with a cymbal-crash. ASQUITH downs his whisky then comes forward as the lights brighten, to address the House of Commons.*]

ASQUITH: I beg that leave be given to introduce a Bill with respect to Military Service in connection with the present war.

1ST MP: [*Recorded.*] Hear-hear!

ASQUITH: The Bill will apply to all male British subjects who have attained eighteen years of age and not yet attained forty-one years of age, and who are unmarried, or widowers without children dependent upon them.

2ND MP: [*Recorded.*] Hear-hear!

ASQUITH: There will, however, be provision made for exemption in certain specific cases, such exemption being applied for to the applicant's Local Tribunal; one such exemption being... on the ground of a conscientious objection to bearing arms.

3RD MP: [*Recorded.*] Shame!

4TH MP: [*Recorded.*] If they're fit they shouldn't be exempted!

[*Booing, cries of 'shame!', and 'Order! Order!' as NARRATOR repositions the crates, to suggest the Local Tribunal at Doncaster. NARRATOR picks up BERT's jacket again and puts it on.*]

BERT: So I get my hair cut and make my way to Doncaster...in order to claim exemption from the Local Tribunal.

CLERK: [*Recorded.*] NEXT!

[*The lights change. BERT Brocklesby stands centre stage facing the members of his Tribunal, which includes people he would have been familiar with, local dignitaries, a shopkeeper, as well as a representative from the military. The words of the Tribunal members are recorded, but BERT responds to them live.*]

CHAIRMAN: Mr. Brocklesby - supposing the enemy were to reach Conisbrough and you and those dear to you were in danger of an aggravated and dastardly attack, would you stand by and see them ripped to pieces?

BERT: As the case is hypothetical I don't see...

CLERK: [*Interrupting.*] Let us have a straight answer. Would your conscience prevent you from striking the enemy down?

BERT: I would certainly not strike them down. No man is justified in taking life.

MILITARY REP: You would stand by and see women and children cut to pieces and not raise a sword in opposition?

BERT: I would do my best to prevent the enemy, but as the case is hypothetical there might be a chance given us of escaping long before.

TOWNSWOMAN: You would run away?

BERT: Certainly.

TOWNSWOMAN: When Germany marched into Belgium was there a chance to run away?

[*An awkward pause.*]

CLERK: How long have you been a schoolteacher, Mr. Brocklesby?

BERT: Certified nearly seven years.

CHAIRMAN: Have you any objection to non-combatant service?

BERT: Yes. I do.

SHOPKEEPER: Is it generally known in your community that you belong to a Brotherhood of some

	fifty or sixty members who will not agree to anything this Tribunal advise or direct?
BERT:	You mean the No-Conscription Fellowship. I have never made a secret about the matter. The membership nationally is now 5,000. Our supporters include prominent figures like Bertrand Russell.
TOWNSWOMAN:	We're not interested in Bertrand Russell.
MILITARY REP:	[*Whispered aside.*] Who's Bertrand Russell?
CHAIRMAN:	Supposing there was a battle just here and you, amongst five or six others at Conisbrough, could save, say, 500 poor women and children by fighting, would you not do your best to save them?
BERT:	I would do my best to save life, but not by taking life.
MILITARY REP:	If you would not exert yourself to defend women and children from being murdered, I think you are just as responsible for the lives of those women and children as if you had taken their lives yourself.
SHOPKEEPER:	Quite right!
CLERK:	It seems he has an objection to doing anything that will take him into danger.
BERT:	I am ready to die for my principles! I am standing up for freedom of conscience of all Englishmen! I cannot bring evidence to prove my conscientious objection.

The only way to prove it is to be ready to suffer for it and if necessary die for it. [*To MILITARY REP.*] You can send me where you will, even into the front-line trenches, but you will never, never, get me to raise my hand against my fellow-man.

[*A pause.*]

TOWNSWOMAN: Are you a local preacher, Mr. Brocklesby?

BERT: Yes, I am.

TOWNSWOMAN: Then I think you had better preach somewhere else.

CHAIRMAN: You will be exempted from combatant service but will be recommended for non-combatant service. Next!

[*A change of light as NARRATOR removes BERT's jacket and puts it on the wooden coat-stand.*]

NARRATOR: Bert Brocklesby was lucky to be given time to state his case. Other objectors had a different story to tell...

[*NARRATOR moves upstage and now portrays various objectors before their Tribunals.*]

1ST TRIBUNAL: [*Recorded.*] Name?

BING: Harold Bing.

1ST TRIBUNAL: [*Recorded.*] Age?

BING: 18.

1ST TRIBUNAL:	[*Recorded.*] 18? Oh in that case, you're not old enough to have a conscience. Case dismissed. Next!
2ND TRIBUNAL:	[*Recorded.*] We gather you're a Socialist?
SOCIALIST:	Yes. I am.
2ND TRIBUNAL:	[*Recorded.*] Well since you're a Socialist you can't have a conscience. Case dismissed. Next!
3RD TRIBUNAL:	[*Recorded.*] What's your religion, young man?
ATHEIST:	I'm an atheist.
3RD TRIBUNAL:	[*Recorded.*] An atheist doesn't have a conscience. Case dismissed!

[*Cries of "Case dismissed! Case dismissed!" As the lights brighten the Pathe-style newsreel music is heard.*]

NEWSCASTER:	[*Recorded.*] April 1916. Clifford Allen, chairman of the No-Conscription Fellowship, addresses their emergency national convention in Bishopsgate Hall, London.

[*NARRATOR moves two crates to form a lectern, then becomes Clifford ALLEN, standing at the lectern addressing the convention.*]

ALLEN:	Friends two years ago, after war had broken out, this conference adopted a statement of faith in which we, an organisation of men who hold every sort of political and religious opinion, vowed two things: firstly, to refuse to bear arms because we consider

human life to be sacred; and secondly, to oppose every effort to introduce compulsory military service into Great Britain.

Sadly, we could not prevent the latter from happening. However, our statement of faith went on to say that should this evil thing conscription be introduced, we would all, whatever the consequences might be, obey our conscientious convictions rather than the commands of government!

NEWSCASTER: [*Recorded.*] 2,000 young men cheer and stamp and bellow their approval, while hostile crowds gathered outside grow ever more incensed. Some even try to break their way into the hall. Fenner Brockway, the N-C F's founder, immediately takes evasive action.

[*NARRATOR puts on BROCKWAY's spectacles.*]

BROCKWAY: Please, please, no applause, please! Might I suggest that we refrain from applauding and cheering loudly at the end of every rousing speech, because as you can hear, that will only exasperate and inflame the crowds gathered outside even more. What I propose instead – if you agree, Clifford? – is that you wave your handkerchiefs. Or should you not have a handkerchief, your white agenda papers?

[*NARRATOR takes the spectacles off and breaks forward to address the audience.*]

NARRATOR: I'm trying to imagine what that must have looked like! Two thousand white handkerchiefs! [*He has an idea.*] In a moment, when the newsreel gives the cue, would you all be up for passionately waving something, your own handkerchief or... the programme maybe? Here we go...

NEWSCASTER: [*Recorded.*] And so speaker after speaker, including Bertrand Russell, who arrives bringing with him a young C.O. he has just bailed from jail, is greeted with a tumultuous sea of handkerchiefs!

[*NARRATOR leads the way as the audience flap their white hankies.*]

NARRATOR: Wow! Thank you...

[*NARRATOR takes up his position behind the lectern again.*]

ALLEN: Friends ... friends ... in a moment I shall read out the names of the first fifteen C.O.s to have been arrested. Every young man in this hall, including Fenner and myself, must realise that we ourselves only have weeks or maybe days before our own freedom is snatched from us!

[*SFX Collage of sound of door-knockers and door-bells. The recorded voices of a POLICEMAN and Bert's father, JOHN.*]

POLICEMAN: [*Recorded.*] Mr. Brocklesby - is your son Bert at home?

JOHN: [*Recorded.*] What do you want him for, officer?

POLICEMAN: [*Recorded.*] This 'ent easy for me, sir – but I've come to arrest him, for failing to answer the summons to join the Non-Combatant Corps.

[*BERT steps forward with the summons.*]

BERT: Of course I don't answer the summons. [*He scrunches it up.*] I haven't agreed to be in any part of the army. So they arrest me... and I'm taken to Richmond Castle.

NARRATOR: I'm pretty sure I would have applied for exemption under the conscience clause, but if it hadn't been granted to me, would I have thrown away the summons?

[*A change of light. The guardroom at Richmond Castle. NARRATOR portrays BERT and an army SERGEANT.*]

SERGEANT: Right, Private Brocklesby, here's a bucket of potatoes and a knife, now get peeling.

[*The SERGEANT picks up a small crate and shoves it onto the ground to represent the bucket.*]

BERT: May I ask who they're for?

SERGEANT: Beg pardon?

BERT: The potatoes? Who are they for?

SERGEANT: They're for the officers and soldiers, who do you think they're for?

BERT: Then I can't peel them, I'm afraid. I'll peel potatoes for conscientious objectors but not for officers and soldiers.

SERGEANT: We're not asking you to kill anybody, Brocklesby, we're asking you to get our supper ready.

BERT: I'm sorry, but I can't do that.

SERGEANT: Well let's see if three days solitary confinement on bread and water will help change tha' mind!

[*SFX of a steel door clanging shut as BERT is shoved onto one of the crates - a stool in his cell. Fade up. SFX Newsreel interplayed with SFX Parliament.*]

SPEAKER: [*Recorded.*] Order! Order! Mr. Philip Snowden... [3]

SNOWDEN: [*Recorded.*] Another case I want to bring to the attention of the House is that of Jack Gray, a conscientious objector just nineteen years of age, who endured days of being abused and beaten up, had a live grenade thrown at his feet and was forced to march with a suitcase filled with stones.

[*The light darkens as NARRATOR acts this out, as Jack Gray, struggling to carry the largest wooden crate around the stage. He drops it, and collapses by it, exhausted, before being hauled to his feet. He then puts a rope over his head.*]

---

3 Philip Snowden (1864-1937) was chair of the Independent Labour Party from 1903-06, the year in which he became Labour MP for Blackburn. Although not a pacifist, Snowden opposed armed forces recruitment and vigorously campaigned against conscription, highlighting injustices and repeating concerns that C.O.s might be taken to France where they could be shot. His stance was unpopular with the public and he lost his seat in the 1918 general election. He returned to the House (in 1922 as MP for Colne Valley) and was Labour's first Chancellor of the Exchequer under Ramsay MacDonald. - MM

> On one occasion he was stripped naked, had a rope tightly fastened round his abdomen, and was then dragged to a filthy pond in the camp grounds...

[*Jack Gray stands on the edge of one of the crates, the rope round his waist.*]

> ...into which he was pushed forcibly and entirely immersed eight or nine times in succession...

[*Jack Gray is plunged into the pond and struggles to breathe and reach the surface.*]

> ...and dragged out each time by the rope...

[*Jack Gray is yanked out of the pond and collapses on the ground.*]

> The pond contained sewage.

[NARRATOR *gets up slowly and removes the rope, while an army* SERGEANT's *voice is heard.*]

SERGEANT: [*Recorded.*] Do you get it now? Do you get it? The absolute insignificance of one individual in a modern army! The Government has handed you over to us, the Military, so we can do just as we like with you!

[*A pause.*]

NARRATOR: [*To the audience, quietly.*] God...if that had happened to me, wouldn't I have just given in? Because Jack Gray did. And who can blame him?

[SFX *a haunting woman's voice is heard singing : 'I Didn't Raise My Boy to be a Soldier...' while NARRATOR becomes BERT again, constructing his cell using the wooden crates, two pallets forming the bed. The song trails off, echoing through the corridors of the prison.*]

BERT: [*To the audience.*] My cell in Richmond Castle is about nine feet long by six feet wide, with just a narrow window giving little light. But in the bottom corner of one of the walls, I notice a hole, where heating pipes must have once run. I go to take a closer look...

[*He does so, lying flat on the ground.*]

...and I find a face staring back at me! [*To the face at the hole.*] What are you doing there?

NORMAN: [*Geordie accent.*] Impersonating a mouse, what do you think? I'm Norman Gaudie.

BERT: Bert Brocklesby.

[*They shake hands through the hole. With a simple turn of the head, NARRATOR portrays both men.*]

Do you fancy some bacon, Norman?

NORMAN: Bacon? You've got some *bacon*?

BERT: Ay, smuggled some in beneath my belt.

NORMAN: Man, that's a beautiful sight.

BERT: And do you fancy a game of chess?

NORMAN:	I do, but last time I played you needed a board and pieces.
BERT:	Well, what do you think this is? [*He produces a chess piece.*] Scotch mist?
NORMAN:	Oh man! Bacon, chess - is it Christmas Day?
BERT:	[*To the audience.*] And so we pass our moves on the chess board back and forth through the hole, as well as our opinions on how far we should carry our disobedience.
NORMAN:	Don't know why you're wearing uniform, man; you won't catch me wearing it.
BERT:	Why not? We have to wear something.
NORMAN:	It's a symbol, Bert. If you wear uniform you're sayin' you're part of the Army, you're part of the war.
BERT:	I don't agree, isn't it what we *do* that matters?
NORMAN:	Whatever they say, whatever orders they give, refuse them all.

[*He stands and becomes the SERGEANT.*]

SERGEANT:	Right, you lot, out for drill!
BERT:	I'm sorry, sergeant – I haven't agreed to be part of the army and so...
SERGEANT:	Well, you ARE part of the Army, Brocklesby, and you will do drill. Ten knee-bends, one,

two – I said, ten knee bends! One, two... Corporal, put Private Brocklesby in the correct position. Now step away, Corporal. [*BERT lets himself topple over.*] Very funny, Brocklesby, get up. I said, GET UP!

[*As the SERGEANT is about to strike him, a LIEUTENANT appears.*]

LIEUTENANT: Sergeant, stand aside.

SERGEANT: [*Saluting smartly.*] Yessir!

LIEUTENANT: Listen here, Private Brocklesby. The fact is you've been refused exemption and have been assigned to the Non-Combatant Corps, and therefore you must obey orders. But none of these orders will involve you in compromising your conscience; you won't be involved in any combat. I mean, don't you think it's rather perverse, you refusing to peel potatoes or do a few knee-bends, while on the other side of the Channel your fellow countrymen are sacrificing their lives or receiving horrific injuries? Now get back to your cell!

[*BERT walks back to his cell.*]

BERT: [*to the audience*] Well. We didn't peel spuds, we didn't do drill ...feels like we've won the first hurdle.

[*SFX the voice of the SERGEANT is heard in the corridor outside the cell.*]

SERGEANT: [*Recorded.*] They should be taken outside and shot like dogs!

[BERT *hears this and freezes, then crouches down and starts drawing on one of the cell walls.*]

BERT: May 22nd... I'm drawing a picture of my fiancée, Annie, with a piece of charcoal I smuggled in... it's two months now since we parted outside West Riding Police Court...

[*Flashback. The lights suddenly brighten to full daylight.*

NARRATOR *stands and comes downstage as* ANNIE.]

ANNIE: Bert, I can't bear this! Seeing my brother Gilbert off I thought my heart would break, but having to say goodbye to you too...

BERT: Courage, my love.

ANNIE: I can't bear how everything's changed.

BERT: I know. Conisbrough feels like an alien town. All geared up for war. Hardly recognise it.

ANNIE: I'm going to miss singing for you in the choir.

BERT: Going to miss hearing you.

POLICE OFFICER: [*Recorded.*] Mr. Brocklesby, have to ask you to come with me now.

ANNIE: Bert, you won't be shot, will you?

BERT: Shot? 'Course I won't be shot, love...

POLICE OFFICER: Mr. Brocklesby!

BERT: Disobedience is only punishable by shooting if it happens on active service... in France.

ANNIE: Oh God. Please don't let them shoot you, Bert, please... please...

[*The light changes back to the dimness of the cell. The SERGEANT reenters, slamming a crate down on the floor to represent the bucket of potatoes and banging one particularly large potato on to BERT's pallet bed.*]

SERGEANT: Right, Private Brocklesby, let's see if you're willing to peel some spuds yet! Didn't you hear me? Shall I say it LOUDER? [*He grabs BERT by the lapels.*] Look, I've had about as much as I can stand of you and your fuckin' conscience! [*He thrusts BERT up against the wall.*] You won't take up a rifle to fight the fuckin' Germans, and you won't take up a knife to peel some fuckin' spuds – what will you fuckin' do?

[*The SERGEANT lets go of BERT, who takes a deep breath before calmly explaining himself.*]

BERT: Nothing that promotes the war effort, I'm afraid.

[*BERT recoils as he is struck by the SERGEANT.*]

Please... don't hit me. Nothing will be achieved by –

[*He is struck again, winces with pain and collapses to his knees over the 'bucket'.*]

> Rather than abusing me with ripe language, rather than beating me with your stick, can we not sit down calmly so I can explain to you what I believe and how I've arrived at...

[*He realises the SERGEANT is now pointing a rifle at him. A tense pause.*]

> I don't believe you're permitted to shoot me. We're not on active service.

[*The SERGEANT points the rifle at BERT's chest.*]

> This is against Army regulations. I need to face a court-martial first.

SERGEANT: FUCK the court-martial! If you don't start peeling potatoes by the time I count to three you'll be pushing up fucking daisies instead. One... two...

LIEUTENANT: [*Quietly.*] Sergeant?

SERGEANT: [*Saluting smartly.*] Yessir!

[*NARRATOR turns and becomes the LIEUTENANT, who has entered stealthily.*]

LIEUTENANT: Stand aside. And report to my office in fifteen minutes. [*He watches the SERGEANT leave before continuing.*] Private Brocklesby. I've some news for you. I've just received orders to send you and your chums to France.

[*A short pause as BERT takes in this news.*]

BERT: France? Can I let my family know I'm going, sir?

LIEUTENANT: I'm afraid not. There isn't time.

[SFX *a burst of French accordion music. NARRATOR picks up crates and does a little dance with them as he repositions them to form firstly a platform for the COMMANDING OFFICER, then a seaside jetty, all in time to the music. The accordion music fades away. France. NARRATOR takes an officer's cap from one of the hessian sacks and becomes the COMMANDING OFFICER.*]

COMM. OFFICER: Let me make one thing clear. Whether you like it or not, you men are here in France as part of the Non-Combatant Corps. You won't be going anywhere near the front but you are now deemed to be on active service. Which means that if you keep up your course of disobedience and insubordination you will be subjected to a court-martial, where, should you be found guilty, the maximum penalty will be applied.

BERT: [*Removing the cap and addressing the audience.*] The Commanding Officer then says something extraordinary.

COMM. OFFICER: [*Cap back on.*] I'm going to give you twenty-four hours leave to think it over. You're at liberty to do as you like: go into Boulogne, visit a restaurant, go to the beach if you wish.

BERT: [*Cap off.*] The beach? Did he say we can go to the beach?

COMM. OFFICER: [*Cap on.*] But when you come back I expect you all to have come to your senses. For God's sake ask yourselves – is this 'protest' of yours really worth losing your lives over?

[SFX *of a music-hall audience erupts over the loudspeakers, singing 'Oh I Do Like to be Beside the Seaside.' BERT tosses the officer's cap away and joins in with the song, dancing along in time to the music.*]

SFX SONG: "Oh I do like to be beside the seaside, I do like to be beside the sea; I do like to stroll along the prom prom prom, Where the brass bands play, tiddly om pom pom..."

[*Sound of the sea gently washing onto the shore. BERT walks along a jetty, breathing the fresh salt air, then shouts out.*]

BERT: Hey lads! Who fancies a cuppa?

[*During the second verse of the song, BERT sets up the crates to suggest a French cafe. He then opens one of the wooden trunks and pulls out a bone-china cup and saucer, and sits down at a 'table'. NARRATOR now portrays four C.O.s sitting at the table: BERT, NORMAN, LEONARD and HOWARD.*]

BERT: Right, now listen, lads, we've had a grand day out, but the fact is we're up against it. You heard what the Commanding Officer said. And you know what the maximum penalty is if we continue to disobey.

NORMAN: Oh, Bert, they won't shoot us, they're just bluffing, man.

BERT: How can you be sure?

LEONARD: I don't see why we have to refuse every little order, anyway. I mean, if we agree to march in step, we're not helping to kill anyone, are we?

NORMAN: We need to be consistent.

LEONARD: But these are trivial things – surely we should make a distinction between orders that have a direct bearing on the fighting, and those that clearly don't?

NORMAN: Be absolute. Refuse them all.

HOWARD: Well, I don't fancy being shot and that's a fact.

NORMAN: They're not *goin'* to shoot us, man – there'd be a reet uproar back home.

BERT: But nobody back home knows where we are, do they, Norman?

HOWARD: Then we should write, alerting them to what's going on!

BERT: Do you think the censor would allow any such letter through?

NORMAN: [*Pulling a postcard from his shirt pocket.*] Well, what about one of these then?

LEONARD: What is it?

NORMAN: Field service postcard. Got it from a soldier. Only thing you can write on it is your name – but they've got all these options you can cross out. Like, 'I am quite well', or, 'I am being sent down to the base.' Then there's a bit about receivin' a letter-

HOWARD: Well that doesn't apply to us, does it?

NORMAN: The options bein', 'I have received no letter from you lately', or, 'For a long time.'

BERT:	Let me have a look at it.

[BERT *takes the postcard and looks long and hard at it.*]

LEONARD:	What are you thinking, Bert?

[BERT *makes deletions, then hands the card back to NORMAN.*]

BERT:	There.
NORMAN:	Oh, no! You've nearly obliterated the whole lot – what good's that?
BERT:	Just read it out, Norman – quietly – the bit that's left.
NORMAN:	"I am being sent to... B."
BERT:	And the other bits.
NORMAN:	"Ou." "Long." How long? That doesn't make sense, man.
LEONARD:	You planning on posting this? 'Cos if we can't work it out, no-one back home will be able to.
BERT:	Come on, chaps, engage your brains.
HOWARD:	I've got it! "I am being sent to Boulong"!
BERT:	Ssh!
HOWARD:	"I am being sent to Boulong!"
BERT:	[*Taking the postcard back and pocketing it.*] Only hope they're as quick as you back home, eh, Howard? Else we're in real trouble.

NORMAN: We're not in trouble, man! All that talk of maximum penalty, he was just bluffing, like.

BERT: You don't know that, Norman! But if he was bluffing, what we've got to decide, before we go back to camp, is whether we're prepared to call his bluff. Whether we're prepared to take this all the way to the last ditch.

[*A pause. BERT looks challengingly at the other three men.*]

Well? Are we?

[*NARRATOR stands up sharply as the lights change, taking the pipe from his pocket, then moving forward as Bertrand RUSSELL. London.*]

RUSSELL: [*To the audience.*] Clifford Allen has just been arrested! Which means it falls to me to take over from him as acting chairman of the No-Conscription Fellowship.

[*He rests his pipe on a crate stage-left, then clears away the tea-cup and saucer, putting them back in the wooden trunk.*]

The organisation is divided into a number of departments: the most important of which is the Records Department - in effect the intelligence arm of the N-C F.

[*He collects a sheaf of papers, waving them in his left hand.*]

This department is the brainchild of an exceptional young woman, who was instrumental in the struggle for–

[*He now takes the papers with his right hand and clasps them to his chest, as he turns and becomes Catherine MARSHALL.*] [4]

MARSHALL: Thank you, comrade, I can introduce myself.

[*To the audience.*] Catherine Marshall. Previously involved in the struggle for women's suffrage; now devoting myself utterly to the cause of the C.O.s.

[*She files the papers, using a small crate as a filing cabinet.*]

I've introduced a system whereby every known conscientious objector has his own record card, regularly marked up with his movements and events of importance in his army or prison career. Each card is duplicated in case the first set should be lost or taken by the police-

RUSSELL: [*To the audience.*] Our offices are constantly being raided by the police.

MARSHALL: Not just our offices, Bertie - no less than 150 N-CF branch officials have had their homes raided.

---

4 Catherine Marshall (1880-1961), was among the most important anti-conscriptionists of WWI. She had played a critical role in the development of political strategy by the National Union of Women's Suffrage Societies (the non-militant wing of the women's suffrage movement), for which she worked almost full-time from 1908-1914. In 1915 she went on to help form the British section of the Women's International League for Peace and Freedom, and when the Military Service Act became imminent she worked for the National Council Against Conscription. By March 1916 she was devoting most of her time and political know-how to rallying support for the No-Conscription Fellowship. When Russell became acting chairman after Clifford Allen's arrest, no-one else still at liberty knew as much about the workings of the N-C F as Russell and Marshall. - MM

[SFX *a telephone rings.*]

Printing presses have been smashed and broken up.

[MARSHALL *answers the phone by picking up* RUSSELL's *pipe and using it as the receiver.*]

Catherine Marshall spea...

[*The stentorian voice of Major-General* WYNDHAM CHILDS *is heard.*] [5]

WYNDHAM CHILDS: [*Recorded.*] In my opinion the N-C F is a pernicious organisation!

MARSHALL: [*Aside to* RUSSELL.] Major-General Wyndham Childs.

WYNDHAM CHILDS: Personally, I believe that those of you in charge of it should be dealt with under the Incitement to Mutiny Act!

MARSHALL: But Major-Gen-...

[*But he has hung up.* SFX *a voice crying out 'Fire!' followed by a volley of rifle shots.*]

MARSHALL: [*To the audience.*] A sound that would be music to the ears of many an officer having to deal with disobedient C.O.s. But that sound has not been heard. Not yet.

[SFX *the ominous sound of a military drum is heard, beating a slow march.*

---

5 Major-General Sir Borlase Elward Wyndham Childs KCMG KBE CB (1876 –1946). In 1916 he was appointed Director of Personal Services at the War Office, in charge of Army discipline and primarily responsible for dealing with conscientious objectors. - MM

[*NARRATOR reassembles the crates to form a tower, tossing a rope onto the ground in front of the tower. The light brightens as BERT steps forward.*]

BERT: Our day at the seaside over, we return to camp, are given orders, and refuse to obey them. But the Army doesn't impose the maximum penalty just yet ...

[*The voice of an ARMY SERGEANT is heard as BERT is grabbed by soldiers and strapped up with the rope to the tower of crates.*]

ARMY SERGEANT: [*Recorded.*] Field Punishment Number One requires the offender's arms to be fully stretched out and tied to a gun-wheel or beam or rope, about five and a half feet high. In addition his feet are tied closely together. He will then stand in this position for two hours every day, up to a maximum of twenty-eight days. Field Punishment Number One was introduced into the army as a substitute for flogging, being considered more humane.

[*The light darkens. BERT's arms are now fully stretched out and tied to the rope. He winces.*]

BERT: You can see why it's more commonly known as crucifixion. It's actually a form of torture. Especially in the case of the shorter men, who are virtually hanging by the wrists. To make matters less comfortable it begins to rain... and a cold wind blows straight across the top of the hill.

[*SFX the sound of wind and rain as BERT endures his crucifixion. A moment of stillness – before NARRATOR breaks forward, dropping the rope, to become Catherine MARSHALL. London.*]

MARSHALL: Bertie! They're in Boulogne! The C.O.s! One of the Richmond men, Brocklesby, sent a postcard to his family, who sent it on to the N-C F, look!

[*She waves BERT's postcard at him.*]

RUSSELL: [*Taking the postcard.*] My goodness. This means they're in serious danger then.

MARSHALL: We must act... [*She addresses the audience while picking up RUSSELL's pipe, still doubling as the telephone, to make a phone call.*] A small delegation consisting of myself... [*Speaks into the phone.*] Catherine Marshall speaking... [*To the audience.*] Bertrand Russell, Philip Morrell and Philip Snowden, Independent Labour Party MP, manage to secure... [*Into the phone.*] ...a meeting with the Prime Minister. Thank you!

[*NARRATOR pockets the pipe and moves upstage to the crucifixion 'tower'. France. SFX the ominous military drum is heard again, as BERT is set free.*]

BERT: We're released from our crucifixion and the Sergeant gives us what he swears is our last chance to knuckle down and obey.

[*He picks up a narrow crate and places it on the ground in front of him.*]

[*Indicating the crate.*] He orders us to pick up a case of bully beef. I start to explain to him, firmly but reasonably that we're sorry but we cannot obey any orders which come from a military...

[*The SERGEANT interrupts him.*]

ARMY SERGEANT: [*Recorded.*] Sorry be damned, you bastard! All of you, you're all idle fucking bastards and the sooner the lot of you are six feet under pushing up the fucking daisies the better, you useless pack of fucking cowards!

[*The SERGEANT takes a deep breath.*]

Now get back to your cells!

[*BERT sits down heavily on the 'case' of bully beef.*]

BERT: Thirty-five of us are now court-martialled, found guilty and sent to punishment barracks to await our sentences.

[*The light brightens as NARRATOR stands and picks up the 'case'.*]

NARRATOR: [*To the audience.*] If I'd been there, and was given one last chance, what would I have done?

[*SFX of Big Ben striking six.*]

Would I have refused to pick up the case?

[*SFX Pathe newsreel. During this, NARRATOR clears the crates, to either side of the stage. He places a sheaf of papers on top of one of them.*]

NEWSCASTER: [*Recorded.*] May 1916: Prime Minister Asquith prepares to set off for Dublin where, the Easter Rebellion having just been crushed, he hopes he will be able to find a solution to the intractable Irish problem.

[*Downing Street.*]

PM's SECRETARY: [*Recorded:*] The Prime Minister will see your delegation now.

[*In the following scene NARRATOR portrays ASQUITH, MARSHALL, MORRELL, SNOWDEN and RUSSELL.*]

ASQUITH: [*Sorting through the sheaf of papers - his documents.*] Ah, do all come in, won't you? This will have to be brief, I'm afraid, as I'm off to Dublin at any moment.

[*NARRATOR immediately interrupts the scene, breaking forward to the audience.*]

NARRATOR: We don't exactly know what's said in this meeting, or who speaks first - is it Catherine Marshall?

[*NARRATOR spins back round as MARSHALL.*]

MARSHALL: We do appreciate how busy you are, Prime Minister, what we're concerned about is this: that in spite of the many assurances that have been given in Parliament, that those who resist conscription will not be liable to the death penalty, there still seems to exist a considerable amount of doubt over this.

ASQUITH: No, no, Miss Marshall, there's no doubt.

NARRATOR: [*Breaking forward to the audience again.*] I imagine Russell is saying nothing, biding his time. Perhaps Morrell speaks now...

MORRELL: But conscientious objectors are being threatened with it on an almost daily basis, Prime Minister.

ASQUITH: By whom?

MORRELL: Officers, soldiers...

ASQUITH: No, Philip, it's quite clear. The death penalty cannot be imposed in this country on anyone resisting conscription. The Army's sentencing powers are quite limited in that respect.

NARRATOR: [*To the audience.*] Still Russell is silent. Perhaps Philip Snowden intervenes...

[*NARRATOR turns and becomes SNOWDEN.*]

SNOWDEN: In this country, yes. But what happens when these C.O.s are taken to France, Prime Minister, into the war-zone, where anyone refusing to obey orders can in fact be subjected to the death penalty?

ASQUITH: [*Irritably.*] I assure you all – *if* any C.O.s *are* ever taken to France, that will not occur.

NARRATOR: [*Breaking forward to the audience.*] It's NOW that I imagine Russell cannot contain himself any longer!

RUSSELL: If? It's not *if!* Why haven't you shown the postcard, Catherine? They're *there*, Prime Minister, they're *there*. In Boulogne. Refusing to obey orders as we speak, perhaps being court-martialled as we speak, possibly being sentenced to death, even, as we speak!

[*A brief pause as ASQUITH, aghast, registers this.*]

ASQUITH: You're certain these men are in Boulogne?

RUSSELL: We've received information, Prime Minister – which is more, I'm afraid to say, than can be said for your government!

[*He slaps down BERT's Boulogne postcard on top of ASQUITH's papers.*]

The fact is, C.O.s are being sent by the Army to France seemingly without anyone's knowledge. God, I wish I wasn't so old! I wish I were of an age I could be called up, and so be arrested and take my stand alongside these fearless young men!

ASQUITH: If casualties continue at the current rate, Russell, you may yet get your wish.

RUSSELL: The point is, will they be shot! Because if these C.O.s are executed, simply because their consciences would not permit them to take up arms against a fellow human being, it will be the greatest stain imaginable on our nation's reputation!

[*SFX the rasping voice of a SERGEANT-MAJOR rips out, as NARRATOR slams down a wooden pallet centre-stage.*]

SGT. MAJOR: [*Recorded.*] Prisonerrrrs! Faaall IN! And... left... left... left... right... left...

[*The light becomes hot. France. Only BERT speaks live in the following scene, all other voices are recorded.*]

BERT: [*To the audience, quietly.*] A week waiting in the punishment barracks, and then finally we're marched to the parade ground at Henriville, high above the sea, to hear our

	sentences read out. Only we don't march. We never do. We just walk.
SGT. MAJOR:	...left an' HALT! [*Aside.*] Bastards!
ADJUTANT:	Private John Hubert Brocklesby - step forward.

[BERT *walks forward, looking around him, before stepping onto the wooden pallet.*]

BERT:	There're a thousand soldiers assembled on three sides of a square; the adjutant on the fourth side, his back to the sea.
ADJUTANT:	Private John Hubert Brocklesby, of the 2nd Eastern Company, Non-Combatant Corps - you have been charged with persistent refusal to obey orders while on active service in France. You have been tried by a field general court-martial and have been found guilty.
BERT:	He pauses. There's a sinking feeling in my stomach... Wondering... What's going to turn up?
ADJUTANT:	Your sentence is as follows.
BERT:	He pauses again. Longer this time.
ADJUTANT:	Death. By shooting.
BERT:	Well... that's that then. I hear someone behind me saying:
ANOTHER C.O.	Christ, if they shoot Methodists, you and me'll be burnt at the stake.

SGT. MAJOR: QUIET!

ADJUTANT: Sentence awaiting confirmation by the Commander in Chief, General Sir Douglas Haig.

BERT: He consults his papers.

ADJUTANT: Sentence... confirmed.

[*A pause.* BERT *quietly steps off the pallet and approaches the audience.*]

BERT: I seem to accept the fact almost without concern. My mind seems to be occupied mechanically and dispassionately with considering the immediate practical effects. [*He imagines seeing his mother to the right of him.*] 'Twill be a great trial for you, mother, won't it? [*He squats down, imagining himself by his father's bedside.*] And father... your health has been so poorly of late. How will you recover from this? [*He turns and looks up at ANNIE, who he imagines has just entered the room.*] Annie... Annie... this will truly break your heart...

ADJUTANT: But afterwards commuted by the Commander in Chief... to penal servitude for 10 years.

[SFX *a high ethereal note is heard, as* BERT *slowly rises, trying to make sense of this.*]

BERT: What? What?

[BERT *steps back up onto the pallet.*]

NORMAN: We've done it, Bert! We've won, man!

BERT: I feel something surging up within me ... joy ... triumph ... *pride!* To be one of this noble army of C.O.s, engaged in the most glorious struggle that has ever been fought – bar NONE.

[*He steps off the pallet, turns and becomes the ADJUTANT.*]

ADJUTANT: [*Spoken live.*] Private Brocklesby. It's a long-standing tradition in the army to acknowledge the courage of the enemy. I think you men ... are very brave men.

[*The ethereal note increases in intensity, as does the light. They then snap off with the clanging shut of a prison door. A snatch of the wartime song: 'I Didn't Raise My Boy to Be a Soldier' now sung by a jaunty male quartet, is heard as NARRATOR clears the wooden pallet to the side and picks up the plank of wood removed from the crate at the start of the play. He then takes RUSSELL's pipe from his pocket, along with a bloodied handkerchief.*

London. RUSSELL, pipe in mouth, enters his flat holding a plank of wood. He sits, opens the wooden trunk and removes a glass of sherry, from which he takes a large sip. He then attends to a wound on his hand, using the bloodied handkerchief.]

RUSSELL: [*To the audience.*] I was at a Peace meeting organized to promote workers' and soldiers' councils, when a drunken mob burst in led by a few police officers. [*He winces as he dabs and dries his wound.*]

Everybody had to escape as best they could while the police calmly looked on. Several women had their clothes torn off their backs, while two drunken viragos began to attack me with boards full of rusty nails.

[*He presents the plank with its rusty nails to the audience, then puts it aside.*]

I was wondering how one defended oneself against this type of attack when one of the ladies among us approached the police and suggested that they should defend me. 'He is an eminent philosopher,' said the lady. The police however merely shrugged their shoulders. 'But he is famous all over the world as a man of learning,' she continued. The police remained unmoved. 'But he is the brother of an Earl!' she cried. At this, the police rushed to my assistance.

[*He wryly toasts the audience as he downs his glass of sherry, placing the glass back inside the wooden trunk. SFX the House of Commons.*]

THE SPEAKER: [*Recorded.*] The Prime Minister!

ASQUITH: [*Recorded.*] The Government is increasingly aware that it can't just deal with the problem of conscientious objectors by locking them all up. Therefore we intend to introduce a scheme. The Home Office Scheme...

[*SFX sound of steady rain. Sound of a stone-breaking machine. BERT repositions the crates to suggest the quarry at Dyce. The two wooden pallets form 'duckboards' across the mud. BERT walks along the 'duckboards', carrying a small crate filled with rocks before tipping it into the machine.*]

BERT: [*To the audience.*] Dyce – a remote village near Aberdeen ... where 250 of us conscientious objectors, released from prison on the grounds that we are genuine, have been sent to break up rocks. Sorry. Sent to do "*work of national importance.*"

[*The C.O.s talk while working.*]

GORDON: [*Brummie accent.*] Hey, Bert - we havin' a concert tonight?

BERT: Tomorrow - tonight's a debate.

GORDON: Oh ah, what's the subject?

BERT: Utopia.

GORDON: Oh, I went there once, for my holidays.

STEPHEN: How was it?

GORDON: Rained all week.

STEPHEN: Just like here then.

[*SFX a SCOTS WARDER speaks through a megaphone.*]

SCOTS WARDER: [*Recorded*]. Less of the blabberin', you lot.

STEPHEN: Hey, warder, we shouldn't have to work in these conditions - all this mud slopping around!

SCOTS WARDER: Och, cease your whinin'!

GORDON: And our tents are leaking - all the bedding and blankets are wet through!

SCOTS WARDER: Be glad you're not in fuckin' France, you'd know about it then. Mud and shite and lice; they dinnae complain, our brave lads out there, risking their lives - not like you bunch of soft bastards!

[*BERT stands and turns to face the WARDER.*]

BERT: What about Walter Roberts?

SCOTS WARDER: Who?

BERT: The lad in the hospital tent, suffering from pneumonia. Don't tell me he's not risking his life.

SCOTS WARDER: My brother died fighting at Loos last year – I couldnae care less about Walter bloody Roberts!

[SFX *a roll of thunder is heard.* BERT *now moves the pallets together to suggest a bed in the hospital tent. He takes a piece of hessian from one of the trunks and throws it over the bed as a 'blanket'.* BERT *enters the tent and crouches down beside Walter's bed.*]

BERT: Walter? Hey up, lad, it's Bert. How you feeling today?

What?

[BERT *notices a leak in the tent above Walter's head.*]

Oh goodness ... these tents, eh? On their last legs! Here, let me move you.

[BERT *gently eases Walter's camp-bed a few inches to one side.*]

There. How's that?

[BERT *bends down so he can hear Walter more easily.*]

What did you say?

How do you know that? You sure that's what they said? Walter? Walter?

[BERT *decides not to press him any further.*]

>Sleep, lad. You're exhausted.

[*BERT rests his hand briefly on Walter's forehead, then re-joins the other men outside the tent.*]

BERT: Hey chaps, guess what these stones are being used for? We're helping build a road to the new military aerodrome! Walter heard the warders talking outside the tent. Well, that's it. I say we should stop work straight away.

[*He meets resistance from some of the C.Os.*]

>No, we didn't! We agreed to do work of national importance, which I thought would mean agricultural or hospital work, not helping build military roads! Don't you see, chaps? They're just trying to wangle us by hook or by crook into their war machine. They call this 'alternative service' – it's a sham! There is NO alternative but to go back to prison and be true to our principles! So who's going to join me? Anyone?

[*He looks around hopefully at the others.*]

>No one?

[*A brief pause, as BERT realises that he is alone in his protest.*]

>Oh well. I wish you all the best, chaps. And sorry I won't be with you tonight... to discuss Utopia.

[As BERT walks away, SFX another thunderclap is heard, followed by the recorded voice of Fenner BROCKWAY.]

BROCKWAY: To all of us, Walter Robert's life and death must be an inspiration.

[BERT hears this, and stops in his tracks.]

BERT: [Almost praying.] Oh no, lad... may you rest in peace... a true martyr to the cause of peace and brotherhood.

[He walks slowly across the front of the stage. SFX a quartet gently singing 'If I Die'. BERT picks up a small crate and then swiftly turns and shoves it down by one of the upstage crates. Maidstone Prison. A SOUR WARDER is escorting BERT to his cell.]

SOUR WARDER: Here y'are, Brocklesby, welcome to Maidstone!

BERT: [To the audience.] The biggest shock is ... we're not allowed to talk. Only after three months of good –

SOUR WARDER: HEY! There's NO TALKING.

[SFX The slam of a cell door. BERT sits on the small crate in silence. As he gazes out of a tiny prison window, rubbing his hands against the cold, we hear his (recorded) thoughts.]

BERT: [Recorded.] Only after three months of good conduct will we be allowed 'talking exercise', as they call it, every Sunday afternoon. And only after five years will we be allowed to talk every day.

There are thirteen hundred of us C.O.s now in prison, who absolutely refuse

                        to compromise or accept any of the
                        Government's schemes. And that's what
                        we become known as – the 'Absolutists'.

[SFX. *The sound of a packed courtroom and the banging of a judge's gavel. London. NARRATOR rises and then sits on a larger crate, upstage centre, becoming the JUDGE.*]

JUDGE: Mr. Russell. The suggestion in your
                        'article' that American soldiers might be
                        employed in this country as strike-breakers
                        is an offensive and despicable one. I have
                        no hesitation therefore in sentencing you
                        to join those others of your disreputable
                        organisation already behind bars for six
                        months!

[*SFX gasps of astonishment are heard. NARRATOR stands and brings the crate to centre stage, now becoming RUSSELL. Brixton Prison.*]

RUSSELL: [*To the audience.*] Fortunately, thanks to the
                        intervention of my friends, I am placed in
                        the first division where I can have my own
                        clothes... and furniture...

[*He opens the wooden trunk and takes out a red tasselled cushion, which he places on the crate.*]

                        ...where I'm given no prison work, and am
                        able to read and write as much as I like,
                        provided I do no pacifist propaganda.

[*He takes a small gilt-framed photograph of Ottoline from the trunk and places it on another crate. He then takes the pipe from his pocket and is about to put it in his mouth, when he stops himself.*]

I'm not allowed to smoke, which is tedious, but I am allowed flowers... ooh... and chocolates.

[*He takes a small box of chocolates from the trunk and offers them to members of the audience.*]

Care for one?

[*He then sits on the cushioned crate.*]

I've already written a book, though it has to be censored first before it can be sent out. It's an 'Introduction to Mathematical Philosophy'. I gather it's been given to the prison chaplain to scrutinise – I wish him luck with that.

I have plenty of time to think, of course, and lately have been asking myself: my work for the C.O.s – hasn't all my effort and agitation on their behalf simply proved fruitless?

[*He stands and picks up the photo of Ottoline.*]

When Ottoline visited last week she assured me that it hasn't. That I've helped achieve a real victory. That thanks to my efforts the lives of C.O.s have been saved. For what, though, I asked her? Years of penal servitude?

[*He mournfully replaces the photograph.*]

What kind of victory is that?

[NARRATOR *stands and becomes Catherine MARSHALL visiting Clifford ALLEN in Wormwood Scrubs Prison. The light darkens and narrows to focus on ALLEN's dingy cell.*]

MARSHALL: Clifford? Clifford?

[NARRATOR *sits on one of the up-ended pallets by the stage-left wall and, as ALLEN, slowly turns his head to look at his visitor.*]

ALLEN: Catherine. How lovely to see you. [*He thinks for a moment.*] I'm not sure... the solitude... it's a greater strain than I could ever have imagined... the endless flow of thoughts and ideas... that you can't share with anybody...can't even commit them to paper... and then you forget them... and next minute, you feel your mind... start chasing after them... it's torture...

[*He looks directly at her.*]

Perhaps I've been wrong, Catherine... perhaps... we should show more charity to those C.O.s who can't be... can't be... [*irritably*] what's the *word*...?

[*She helps him.*]

Absolutists, indeed... mustn't push men to undertake more than they can manage.

[*He becomes conscious of his frail arms.*]

Yes, I've lost a little weight. How's Fenner coping with his imprisonment... have you seen him?

[*NARRATOR jumps up and becomes Fenner BROCKWAY singing in Lincoln Jail:*]

BROCKWAY: "The workers' flag is deepest red, It shrouded oft our martyred dead!"

[*To the audience, as he waves the red cushion and clears away the crate from centre-stage.*]

I consistently *refuse* to obey their wretched Rule of Silence...

"And ere their limbs grew stiff and cold, Their hearts' blood dyed its ev'ry fold."

For which I am consistently subjected to solitary confinement.

[*He is bundled out of his cell and thrown into a much smaller one.*]

[*To the warders.*] But whatever hole you put me in – you cannot stop me SINGING!

[*At the top of his voice, joyously.*] "Then raise the scarlet standard high! Within its shade we'll live or die.

Though cowards flinch and traitors sneer, We'll keep the Red Flag flying here!"

[*London. N-C F Office. Catherine MARSHALL reads the following letter to herself while we hear BERT'S recorded voice.*]

BERT: Dear Miss Marshall. The members in our prison have been vigorously debating whether or not to carry out a work strike. Could the National Committee signal its wishes to us by flying a flag on the third tree in the avenue outside the prison walls. A red flag for the strike, a white one against.

MARSHALL: I'm not sure I'm up to climbing a tree. [*Looking round at her colleagues.*] Is anyone else in the office? No... and anyway, what if we're interrupted by an intrusive policeman?

[*She sees something through the window.*]

Just a moment. I've had an inspiration.

[*SFX a windy day. Bright daylight. Catherine MARSHALL is flying kites with children outside Maidstone Prison.*]

Children! Fly them over here, there's more breeze here. That's it! [*She eagerly eyes the 'target' tree.*] Oh! Has it got stuck in the tree? Hard luck... No, no, don't try and pull it free, I'll give you another one... here... [*She takes a white handkerchief from her pocket, representing the kite, and shows it to the child.*] No, I'm afraid we've only got white kites...

[*She 'flies' the kite, gently waving the white handkerchief from side to side, then higher and higher, until it gets 'caught in the tree', represented by MARSHALL holding it up high, leaving it dangling from her left hand.*]

[*To the audience.*] The signal is received just in time and the National Committee's decision is passed round the prison - silently of course, talking being forbidden - that there are to be <u>no</u> work strikes.

[*The light fades back to the interior gloom of Maidstone Prison workshop. BERT repositions crates to suggest work-tables, with smaller crates acting as benches beside them. The men work in silence. BERT is stitching a repair to a white handkerchief.*]

BERT: [*To the audience, in a dry, hoarse voice*] As the weeks roll into months, and the months roll into years, our voices become rusty from lack of use... but on the other hand we do become expert tailors. [*He holds up the handkerchief.*] It's November 1918, and all kinds of rumours are flying about...

SOUR WARDER: Brocklesby! Telegram for you!

NORMAN: What is it, Bert? You being released?

SOUR WARDER: Quiet!

BERT: [*Lowering his voice.*] No. [*He opens the telegram.*] It's my fiancée, Annie...

[*SFX The recorded voice of ANNIE is heard.*]

ANNIE: My dear Bert, I wanted to let you know that we've just had news... that my brother Gilbert has been killed in action. It seems a faulty shell exploded just as his gun crew fired it...

[*BERT stands and moves slowly upstage with the telegram. SFX an explosion, then another, shading into fireworks, bells, horns, building in number and volume.*

London. NARRATOR comes downstage as Bertrand RUSSELL, pipe in hand.]

RUSSELL: When the Armistice is announced, I'm in Tottenham Court Road. Within two minutes everybody in all the shops and offices is flooding into the street. Some are commandeering the buses, making them go just where they please. I see a man and woman, complete strangers to each other, meet in the middle of the road...and kiss.

I feel strangely solitary amid the rejoicings, like a ghost dropped from another planet. Of course, I too rejoice at the news, but I can find nothing in common between my rejoicing and that of the heaving, dancing crowd...

[SFX *a burst of music and revelry as a crowd is heard singing 'God Save the King', while NARRATOR jigs round the stage, repositioning the crates to form a different workspace. He tosses a shoe high into the air, catches it, then sits down on a crate, as BERT.*]

BERT: April 12th. 1919.

[*Maidstone Prison workshop. BERT is repairing a shoe.*]

[*Almost to himself.*] When the day comes they eventually let us out of here, I think I might become a cobbler.

NORMAN: There's somethin' I could say to that, but I won't.

SOUR WARDER: Quiet! You, Brocklesby, a cobbler? What do you know about footwear? Fact is, you'll have trouble finding any kind of work, you lot! Wait till you read the papers and look at the small ads. Here y'are: "Vacancy for Teaching Post, Maidstone School for Boys... C.O.s need not apply." Or how about this? "Tailor's Assistant Required..."

NORMAN:	Oh, we could do that, Bert. We've had nearly three years' experience!
SOUR WARDER:	"C.O.s need not apply."
BERT:	Well, once we do get out we'll be voting to change all that - do away with such petty prejudice.
SOUR WARDER:	Quiet! You lot won't be voting for no-one - aintcha' heard? Conchies have been barred from voting for five years. If it was up to me, you'd be barred for life!
BERT:	[*To the audience.*] And then the door to the workshop opens. Another warder appears - all he says is:
2ND WARDER:	Brocklesby, Gaudie, Murfin wanted!
BERT:	Is this it, Norman? Are we being released? [*To the audience, as puts the shoe down on the work-table.*] We're taken out and told to collect our few things, books and photos - I say to him: What about that shoe?
2ND WARDER:	Which shoe?
BERT:	[*BERT picks up the shoe again, almost unable to part from it.*] The shoe I'm repairing; haven't finished it yet...
2ND WARDER:	[*Grabbing the shoe and tossing it away.*] Oh, forget the shoe, just move will you!

[*BERT walks through the corridors of the prison.*]

BERT: [*To the audience.*] And then we're marched back along the corridor... it is, it's happening, we're being released... men are standing by their cell doors watching us, they start drumming their feet...

[*SFX the drumming of feet is heard.*]

...softly at first but then ever more insistently, swelling higher and higher, rolling along the corridors of that house of pain... it's against all the rules but the warders can't stop them... the sound of it... it grips my heart and almost makes me weep.[6]

[*The drumming of feet suddenly stops. The gloom of the prison is dispersed. London. The closing conference of the N-C F in 1919.*]

MARSHALL: [*To the audience.*] After three prison sentences, dear Clifford is now a frail and emaciated thirty-year-old who looks twice his age, and is suffering from the onset of tuberculosis...

[*NARRATOR turns and becomes a frail Clifford ALLEN approaching the lectern. When he speaks his voice is weak.*]

ALLEN: Friends... three years ago we stood in this hall and made a pledge to resist conscription. Not one of us would dare

---

6 We published *This Evil Thing* on 12 April 2017, 98 years to the day after Bert Brocklesby's release from prison. "April 12th, 1919, was our day of liberation," Bert wrote in his memoir, "to the great annoyance of those who were still waiting to see their boys demobbed from the army." After the end of the war, the government was far more concerned about demobilising disgruntled soldiers than it was in looking after conscientious objectors. It was Churchill who managed to persuade the Cabinet, in April 1919, to allow almost all of them home. - MM

> to compare the suffering we subsequently underwent with that of the men who were actually engaged in warfare.

[*He coughs painfully, but then gathers strength from somewhere deep within himself.*]

> But we are proud to have broken the power of the military authority. We have witnessed at first hand its brutalities. We have seen the cruel degrading of human personality upon which its discipline depends. But we have defeated that authority! And should this evil thing conscription continue, we will defeat it again!

[*SFX Thunderous applause, growing in volume, then fading away... as NARRATOR walks over to the wooden coat-stand, takes BERT's jacket, and puts it on again.*]

BERT: [*To the audience.*] Prison warder was right though... finding work doesn't prove easy, especially in my home town. But then I get this idea, which I want to share with Annie...

ANNIE: Vienna! You're going to go to Vienna?

BERT: The Quakers are setting up an organisation there, you see – to help feed the children in the city, they're suffering terribly, there're so many orphans. And so yes, I'm thinking of joining them. And I'd very much like you to come with me, Annie. [*He approaches her, smiling warmly.*] And when we return, well, then we could get married.

ANNIE: [*Turning away from him.*] Those are the people that killed my brother!

BERT:	Annie... it wasn't the children of Vienna who killed your brother.
ANNIE:	You've been away from the world too long – you've no idea what we've endured these last years!
	[*Moving away from him now.*] Don't take my hand, Bert, I'm in no mood to –
BERT:	Please, Annie, don't be angry with me –
ANNIE:	Of course I'm angry! Why wouldn't I be angry at such a... such a proposal as that!

[*She shakes her head in despair.*]

    You ask too much.

[*A pause. She fingers her engagement ring.*]

    You'll have to come to a decision, Bert. Whether you want to spend your life with me, here in England, or go with the Quakers to work in Vienna. You won't be able to do both.

BERT: Well. That's a staggerer.

[*BERT steps forward.*]

    [*To the audience.*] For a moment, I think about tossing a coin again... help me decide...

[*He takes out the coin he'd borrowed from the audience member earlier.*]

    ...but I don't.

[*He hands the coin back to the audience member.*]

> I know where my future lies.

[*With a final glance at ANNIE, BERT walks away.*]

[*SFX The high ethereal note from the parade-ground earlier is heard again as NARRATOR takes off BERT's jacket, letting it fall into an open crate upstage, before turning back to the audience.*]

NARRATOR: More than 16,500 young British men refused to act against their consciences. 31 of those lost their sanity, and at least 70 were known to have died while in the hands of the military.

[*He stands three of the crates on end. They now resemble headstones.*]

> 70! It's a tiny number compared to the 19,240 British soldiers who lost their lives on the first day of the Battle of the Somme...

[*He stands two more crates on end. Two more headstones.*]

> ...and whose courageous sacrifice is remembered every Armistice Day.

[*With the two pallets on end upstage resembling a fence and entrance gate, the positioning of the crates now suggests that we are in a war cemetery. SFX A gentle lament is heard, sung by the same woman whose voice was heard in the prison corridors earlier - a variation on 'The Last Post' - as NARRATOR collects a final crate and carries it on his shoulder slowly and solemnly to a spot downstage centre, carefully placing it to complete the image of the cemetery.*]

He kneels by it and takes RUSSELL's bloodied handkerchief from his pocket, placing it on the headstone in the shape of a poppy. After a moment he stands again.]

> But the question I want to ask is this - the young men who showed a different kind of courage, *refusing* to fight whatever punishments were thrown at them, passionately believing that this was the best, indeed the *only* way to truly serve the cause of peace... aren't they equally worthy of being remembered?

[The woman's gentle sung lament is still heard as NARRATOR goes and sits at the side of the stage.]

> And there's the other question, of course - how would *I* have responded if I'd been a young man in 1914?
>
> Would I have had the courage to endure solitary confinement, crucifixion, the threat of execution... immersion in a pond full of sewage... imprisonment in a ten feet deep pit?

[He picks up the remaining crate from the first scene of the play - the 'pit' - and places it amongst the other 'headstones', then stands directly behind it.]

> I truly hope I *would* have had the courage.

[He steps onto the crate, into the 'pit', decisively. Then is struck by a quiver of doubt.]

> But there's no way of knowing. Is there?

[The sung lament gently increases in volume before fading into silence. Far above, the sound of skylarks is heard. The man in the pit looks up in surprise,

then stretches his hand out, pointing towards the distant birds, towards the light, which grows in intensity.]

The 70

Peter ALLEN
Thomas ALLEN
Walter Charles ALLEN
A BARLOW
Frederick BATTERHAM
Harold BEYNON
Walter BONE
F BOWDEN
Alfred George BRENTNALL
Oliver Stanley BRIDLE
Harold BRIGHTMAN
William Edward BURNS
Arthur BUTLER
Thomas CAINEY
Alexander Neil CAMPBELL
Peter CAMPBELL
Charles John COBB
Ernest H CROSBY
George Henry DARDIS
Lawrence DELLER
Percy DUXBURY
Alfred E EUNGBLUT
John Llewellyn EVANS
R Glyn EVANS
Henry William FIRTH
Paul Leo GILLAN
Harry GOULDSBOROUGH
Percy HALL
Henry HASTON
Andrew HENDERSON
Harold HOAD
Reginald O HOOPER
Arthur HORTON
William HURLEY

A HURST
Harold Marshall HURST
John Theodore JACKSON
Albert Leverson JAMES
Hubert Thomas Edward JAMES
Sidney LINSCOTT
William Watson MALCOLM
Alfred Matthew MARTLEW
Thomas Darling MATCHETT
William MAY
- MOSS
Joseph MOUNTFIELD
William H PARKIN
Frank Lloyd PARTON
Alexander F PEDDIESON
Harry PHIPPS
Royle Annesly RICHMOND
James Arthur RIGG
Walter Leslie ROBERTS
Albert E RUDALL
Arthur John SLATER
Norman Harris STAFFORD
William STANTON
Alfred Ernest STATTON
William SWETTENHAM
John TAYLOR
Charles Henry THOMPSON
Guy Edwin Laurence TOD
Bennett Henry WALLIS
Westgarth WHINNERAH
Percy A WHITMORE
Frederick John Longley WILKINSON
Arthur WILSON
John George WINTER
Ernest WOODWARD
C ZACHNIES

and there were more...

Recommended Further Reading

Objection Overruled by David Boulton
Bertrand Russell: A Pacifist At War edited by Nicholas Griffin
The Autobiography of Bertrand Russell 1914-1944
Conscription and Conscience by John W Graham
We Will Not Fight by Will Ellsworth-Jones
Comrades In Conscience by Cyril Pearce
Telling Tales About Men by Lois S. Bibbings
Conscientious Objection by Jo Vellacott
The Church of England and the First World War by Alan Wilkinson
We Did Not Fight: 1914-18 experiences of war resisters edited by Julian Bell, with a foreword by Canon H. R. L. 'Dick' Sheppard, who founded the Peace Pledge Union in 1935

Further Acknowledgements

To Tony Simpson at the Bertrand Russell Peace Foundation for his advice and support in seeking permissions to use some of Bertrand Russell's writings, for which permission many thanks are due to Sarah Davey at Taylor and Francis Group.

To Jill Gibbon, grand-daughter of Bert Brocklesby, for seeking the family's approval for use of parts of Bert's story in the play.

To Cyril Pearce and Lois S. Bibbings.

To Ben Copsey and Symon Hill and all at the Peace Pledge Union.

To Dr. Jim Walsh at Conway Hall, London.

To Bruce Kent.

To the Library and librarians at Friends House, London.

To Gareth Machin, artistic director at Salisbury Playhouse, for his support and encouragement throughout the development of the piece.

To Jerry Williams for artwork, leaflet and poster design.

To Simon Richardson for production photography (simonrichardson.org).

Original Illustrations by Carys Boughton

Bert Brocklesby	-	page 5
Bertrand Russell	-	page 8
Fenner Brockway	-	page 14
Clifford Allen after his 3 prison sentences	-	page 18
Catherine Marshall	-	page 88
Walter Roberts	-	page 91

Also published by 49Knights

SHAKESPEARE, HIS WIFE, AND THE DOG
by Philip Whitchurch
(ISBN 978-0-9931975-4-3)

April 1616. Shakespeare has returned to Stratford a rich famous and successful man but all's not well. Why is he so unhappy? Why can't he sleep? Why is his wife furious with him? Who is Will waiting for and why can't Anne find the dog? The secrets, lies, resentments and passions of a marriage laid bare. A sleepless night in Stratford, the one hour traffic of our play.

★★★★★

"A Bardian trainspotter's delight... this is a script which will belong to the ages" - *FringeReview*

"A joyous celebration of Language." - *The List*

★★★★★

PHILIP WHITCHURCH is an actor, director and writer. His film credits include *The English Patient*, *Blue Ice*, *Wondrous Oblivion* as well as *Beowulf and Grendel*.

Philip is well known to TV audiences as *The Bill's* Chief Inspector Philip Cato, Captain William Frederickson in *Sharpe*, and the neighbour, Tyler, in *My Hero*. From 1987 he narrated the children's television classic *The Shoe People*.

His West End credits include: The Inspector in *An Inspector Calls*, *The Changing Room*, *Ghost Stories* and the Dad in the musical *Billy Elliot*, a role he reprised on Broadway. Philip has also worked at the National Theatre, The Globe and the Royal Shakespeare Company.

This script is published by 49Knights

49KNIGHTS
ABOUT US

49Knights was established to do for play scripts what the fair trade movement has done for tea and coffee - to reduce the distance between the producer and the consumer so as to bring maximum reward to the producer and and maximum quality to the consumer. The artists we collaborate with retain 100% ownership of their work and the performance rights. Getting published with 49Knights empowers writers to reach new audiences both in print and on stage.

Our approach to content is inspired by Ben Jonson's 1616 *Folio*. Jonson was the first English playwright to edit his plays to be read as well as performed. We hope that the result is as immersive an experience as seeing the scripts performed live. As publishers, our job is to be the studio sound engineer, getting the artist on record with a minimum of distortion and distraction. It's vital to the integrity of each project that the artist makes all the artistic decisions - it's their voice that matters